Cornerstones of Freedom

Thomas Edison

Nicholas Nirgiotis

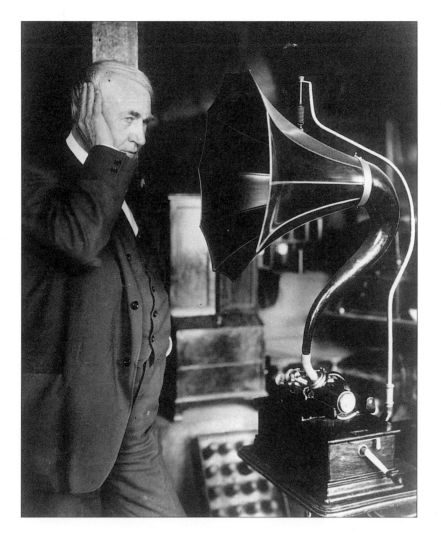

CHILDRENS PRESS®

CHICAGO

Library of Congress Cataloging-in-Publication Data

Nirgiotis, Nicholas.
    Thomas Edison / by Nicholas Nirgiotis.
        p. cm. – (Cornerstones of freedom)
    ISBN 0-516-06676-5
    1. Edison, Thomas A. (Thomas Alva), 1847-1931–
Juvenile literature. 2. Inventors–United States–
Biography–Juvenile literature. 3. Electric engineers–
United States–Biography–Juvenile literature.
    [1. Edison, Thomas A. (Thomas Alva), 1847-1931.
    2. Inventors.] I. Title. II. Series.
    TK140.E3N53 1994
    621.3'092–dc20   93-37028
    [B]   CIP
                                                                      AC

Thomas Edison's "invention factory" in the tiny New Jersey village of Menlo Park was a wonderful place to work. Up-to-the-minute milling machines, microscopes, galvanometers and other electrical apparatus, every known chemical, and thousands of science books made it the best research laboratory in America in the 1870s. Away from the bustle and noise of the city, Edison could think out new ideas and do what he did best—invent new things.

One invention Edison was working on in 1878 was a practical electric light. Electric lighting was not a new idea. Arc lamps (in which a current of electricity leaps across the gap between two carbon points) had been used to light some streets in Europe. But their light was too bright to be used in small spaces. The race was on in the United States and in Europe to invent an electric light that could be used in homes and offices, and Thomas Edison was determined to win.

In September of that year, Edison decided to take a chance. He desperately needed money to pay for his experiments. So he invited a New York newspaper reporter to Menlo Park and announced that he was close to developing a

practical electric light. There were some problems to be worked out, he admitted, but the lamp he had designed worked well.

Edison showed the reporter his incandescent lamp, a glass bulb with a thin platinum wire loop, called a filament, in its center. When electricity from a battery heated the filament, it glowed with a bright white light. The problem was that the platinum filament was very expensive, and it lasted only minutes before burning out. Playing it safe, Edison turned the switch off before the reporter could see the light go out.

The gamble worked. A story praising his work brought Edison the investment money he needed to continue his search for an inexpensive filament that would burn longer than platinum. The key was finding a substance with high electrical resistance so that a small amount of current would keep it burning brightly and steadily. Such a lamp would be cheaper than the gas or kerosene lamps in use at the time.

Edison and his assistants worked without pause through the winter of 1879 to find the right filament. Copper, steel, zinc, nickel, and many other metals and their alloys were cut and placed inside a glass bulb. More than 1,500 different materials were tested in all. Each time, Edison had to pump as much air out of the bulb as he could so that the oxygen would not speed

Thomas Edison
as a young man

One of Edison's assistants testing an early version of the lightbulb

up the burning of the filament. But none of the
materials he tested worked.

So many failures might have made anyone else
give up. Thomas Edison, however, had the
patience and the energy to carry on his work.
Each failure meant simply that what he was
trying to do couldn't be done that particular way.
He would have to find some other way to do it.

By early fall, 1879, Edison was able to obtain
an improved vacuum pump that removed all the
air from the bulb. He also had a new idea. As was

To find the perfect filament for his incandescent lamp, Edison heated various materials until they turned to carbon.

his habit, he had been working on a number of other inventions at the same time. He had just used carbon to improve the telephone. Why not try this material as a filament? The difficulty was getting a long, very thin piece of carbon. Edison's solution was to take a piece of ordinary cotton sewing thread, place it in a metal mold shaped like a hairpin, and heat it in an oven to carbonize it. The most difficult part was attaching the filament to the electrical wire inside the bulb without breaking it.

After several painstaking tries, he succeeded in placing a carbon filament inside the small glass bulb. The new lamp glowed for forty-five hours before burning out. Yet Edison was not quite satisfied. A filament made of carbonized cardboard worked even better. It lasted nearly two hundred hours. Edison's genius and hard work had given the world the first usable electric lamp—what we know today as the lightbulb. It was the beginning of the age of electricity.

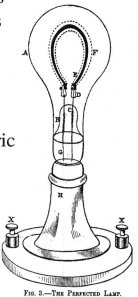

FIG. 3.—THE PERFECTED LAMP.

A. The Vacuum Globe. B. Interior Glass Crest, through which Wires pass to Light. C. Platinum Wires. D. Platinum Clamp. E. Carbonized Cardboard. F. Dotted Line, showing Size of Incandescence equal to Sixteen Candles. G. Copper Wire to Metre and Generator. H. Wooden Stand. X X, Binding Posts.

Fifty years later, Edison reenacts the moment of perfecting the first practical electric light (shown above in a diagram and a photograph).

The electric light was the first step. Now Edison had to supply people using his lamp with the electricity to make it work. Over the next few years, he built generating stations and established electrical distribution networks to bring power to homes and businesses. Devices we use every day—such as safety fuses, switches, sockets, and meters to measure the amount of

After inventing the lightbulb, Edison designed and built generating stations to bring electric power to homes and businesses.

Before long, workers were laying underground wires to carry electricity from central generating stations to streets and homes.

current being used—did not exist then. He had to invent them all.

The invention of the practical electric light made Edison one of the most famous people in the world. People believed he could do anything, and newspapers nicknamed him the "Wizard of Menlo Park." Who was this brilliant man and what was the story of his life?

In 1837, Thomas Edison's father, Samuel, fled from Canada to the United States after taking part in a rebellion against the Canadian

The house in Milan, Ohio, where Thomas Edison was born

government. Soon afterwards, he sent for his wife, Nancy, and his six children. They settled in Milan, Ohio, where Samuel set up a mill to produce roof shingles.

It was in Milan that Thomas Alva, the youngest Edison child, was born on February 11, 1847. Thomas, known as Al when he was young, was an unusual boy. He was restless and mischievous and full of curiosity. He took an interest in everything going on around him, and he especially wanted to know how things worked.

"What makes birds fly?" Al would ask. "How does water put out a fire? How does a hen hatch chickens?" There was no end to his questions. Many people found this a nuisance, but his mother always had the patience to try to satisfy his desire to know.

Her explanations were usually not enough. Al had to try things out for himself. But his experiments did not always turn out well. Once he tried to hatch eggs by sitting on them. Another time he set fire to the barn "just to see what it would do." He nearly burned the house down, and his father punished him by spanking him in public.

Al started school in Port Huron, Michigan, where the Edison family moved after Samuel's business failed in Milan. In the one-room schoolhouse Al attended, students learned by memorizing facts and repeating them. When they failed to do so, or when they were not attentive in class, they were punished.

Al was used to learning in his own way, by doing and making things and by experimenting and asking questions. But his teachers thought he asked too many "foolish" questions, and they decided the boy's mind must be "addled" (confused). There was little hope, they felt, that he would amount to anything.

This was a difficult time for Al. He was always at the bottom of the class, and he felt his teachers did not understand him. His mother, however, believed in him, and was furious at his teachers. Mrs. Edison knew her son was bright. She had been a schoolteacher in Canada before her marriage, and so she decided to take him out of school and teach him herself.

Mrs. Edison believed that children should have fun while learning. She taught Al how to read and write and she helped him study the things that interested him. Best of all, she encouraged him to experiment. When Al was nine, his mother bought him a book on physical science. Al tested every experiment described in the book in his basement laboratory, which was crammed with flasks, wires, scraps of metal, tubes, and chemicals.

Al was grateful for the freedom his mother gave him and he worked hard. Years later, he said, "My mother was the making of me. She let me follow my bent."

In 1859, the Grand Trunk Railroad came to Port Huron from Detroit. Though Al was just twelve years old, he and his parents decided that he should go to work as trainboy on the railroad. In those days, it was not unusual for young people to begin work at an early age.

Al did not mind going to work. His job gave him a chance to see the world and learn how to take care of himself. Each morning at 7:00, he boarded the train at Port Huron for the run to

A Michigan train station in the 1800s

Detroit. Moving from car to car, he sold the passengers candies, snacks, tobacco, and newspapers—items he had bought with his own money. Any profit he made was his to keep.

The train arrived in Detroit about 10:00 each morning and left for the return trip to Port Huron at 6:30 in the evening. Al had plenty of time in between to concentrate on his main interest. He talked the conductor into allowing him to set up a lab in a corner of the baggage car, and spent all his free time there doing experiments. This special favor ended when a piece of phosphorus fell out of its jar and set the car on fire. Al and the conductor put out the blaze quickly, but Al's chemicals went out of the train at the next station.

When Al was twelve, he began selling newspapers and snacks on the train running between Detroit and Port Huron.

Al's job was steady, but it gave him few opportunities to make good money. One such chance came his way on April 6, 1862. The United States was in the midst of the Civil War, and that day, the *Detroit Free Press* carried news of the Battle of Shiloh. Edison talked the editor of the newspaper into giving him 1,000 copies on credit. Then he asked a telegrapher friend to alert operators in towns ahead that the paper with news of the battle would be on the train. When he arrived at each station, there were throngs of people waiting to pay double and triple the price for a copy.

Edison went home that night with his pockets filled with money. But something even more important had happened that day. Edison realized what a marvelous invention the telegraph was. The telegraph worked by sending an electric current through a wire. By using a combination of short and long bursts of current to represent letters of the alphabet, telegraphers could send messages over long distances with great speed. Edison decided he wanted to be part of the exciting new field of telegraphy.

He got his chance when he saved the child of the stationmaster at Mount Clemens, Michigan, from being crushed by a train as he was playing on the tracks. To show his appreciation, the stationmaster taught Al telegraphy. Early in 1863, Edison landed a job as a night telegraph operator at a train station. His job was to alert stations up

Telegraphers in the 1800s

and down the line about the passage of trains.

Edison liked his work. But he was more interested in improving the telegraph than in using it, and when he was sixteen, he made his first useful invention. Night telegraphers were required to send a signal (the number 6) every half hour to prove they were awake on the job. During Edison's entire shift, only one train passed in each direction, and he saw no reason why he should have to be alert the rest of the time. He spent his days reading and tinkering, and needed some rest at night. So he connected a clock to the operator's switch and hooked it up so that the signal was sent out automatically at the right time. Undisturbed, he continued to enjoy his naps—until a suspicious supervisor dropped in at the station without warning.

Edison working on improving the telegraph

Edison's first patented invention, a vote recorder

Edison left his first job and drifted to many others, but inventing remained his most important goal. By the time he was nineteen, in 1866, Al had developed a device that repeated a telegraph signal automatically and another one that increased the distance a message could travel. He also began working on a system that would send two messages at the same time over the same line. In 1868, while working as a telegrapher in Boston, he invented a vote-recording machine. This was Edison's first real invention, and he patented it in 1869. A patent, granted by the government, gives an inventor the exclusive legal right to make, use, or sell his invention for a given number of years.

After the Civil War ended in 1865, large industries began to develop in the United States.

Machines were now doing the work of men. New and improved machines were needed to keep up with the demand. It was a great time to be an inventor, and Thomas Edison was ready to go to work. He had a boundless imagination and believed he could solve any problem. He left Boston in May 1869, and headed for the business capital of the nation.

In New York City, Thomas Edison made the most important decision of his life. He would take the risk of becoming a full-time inventor, but he would invent only things that had practical uses. He would stop drifting from job to job and he would stop being a dreamer and a tinkerer. Unfortunately, at the time, he was a penniless inventor. So he borrowed a dollar from a friend, and lived on that for several days. Meanwhile, he began calling on companies that might be interested in his talents. The chief engineer of the Gold Indicator Company had no job to offer, but allowed Edison to sleep free in the cellar of the company offices. This turned out to be a lucky break for Edison.

The Gold Indicator Company produced and distributed telegraphic machines that sent the latest information about gold prices directly from the Stock Exchange to brokers' offices. These machines were called tickers because of the sound they made. Three days after Edison's arrival, the company's central transmitter broke

Shortly before leaving Boston in 1869, Edison (left) invented an improved version of the stock ticker (right).

down. Edison, having invented an improved version of the stock ticker just before leaving Boston, had no problem fixing the company's machinery. As a reward, he was offered the job of assistant engineer. Later, he improved the machinery so that all the tickers served by the company could be adjusted from the central office whenever they began to print wildly, as they often did. For this invention he was paid $40,000—a huge sum of money in those days.

Thomas Edison could now afford to buy the equipment and hire the assistants he needed to help him continue inventing. At the American

Telegraph Works he set up in Newark, New Jersey, he headed a large team of skilled people who worked on more than two dozen projects at one time. But it was Edison's genius that guided the team.

Edison spent long hours in his workshop, supervising his staff, reading the thousands of books he had collected, experimenting, dealing with businessmen, and taking out patent after patent. At times he found solutions by thinking through a problem. At other times he experimented, endlessly trying different ways or

Edison's Newark invention factory in 1873

Edison was a great inventor because he had the determination to keep working on a problem until it was solved. He never questioned whether something might be done, only how.

materials until he found the right one. He was a good example of his most famous saying: "Genius is one percent inspiration and ninety-nine percent perspiration." One of his greatest strengths was his ability to take advantage of "happy accidents"; when something unexpected happened, he did not hesitate to stop whatever he was doing and turn off course in a new direction.

Busy as he was, in 1871 he found time to marry one of his workers, Mary Stilwell, and to start a family. He playfully nicknamed the first

Clockwise from top left: Edison's first wife, Mary; Edison with his second wife, Mina, and their three children in 1907; Edison and Mina

two of their three children Dot and Dash, the short and long signals used by telegraphers. Mary died in 1884, and in 1886, Edison married Mina Miller. With Mina, Edison had three more children.

In Boston, Edison had worked for Western Union, the largest American telegraph company, and in Newark he continued to make improvements on the telegraph. Among them was the quadruplex, which made it possible to send four messages over the same line at the same time. It was one of the most important

Edison in his Menlo Park laboratory

inventions in telegraphy, and Western Union quickly bought it from him for $30,000.

Despite the inventions and patents pouring out of his shop, Edison was usually short of money because he spent whatever he made buying expensive new equipment and hiring new workers. By this time, Edison's work had become so well known that his Newark workshop was often filled with visitors. To escape all the attention, in 1876 Edison built a laboratory at Menlo Park, New Jersey. It was here that he made some of his most important inventions.

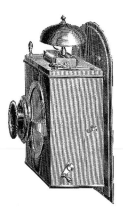

Edison improved the telephone by inventing a better transmitter.

One of his first projects at Menlo Park was improving the telephone, which had just been invented by Alexander Graham Bell. After testing nearly two thousand materials, Edison found that a transmitter made of carbon increased the distance sound could be carried and made reception clearer. This was an important step in making the telephone a practical instrument.

Edison was such a quiet, reserved person that few people knew about the disability that made his work on the telephone and on other inventions difficult. As a child, his hearing had been damaged by scarlet fever and ear infections, and the loss became worse as he grew older. So

Edison and a group of his assistants at Menlo Park in 1880

when he needed to know how a material sounded as a voice transmitter, he depended on his assistants to help him.

But Edison was able to turn even his hearing impairment into an advantage. For one thing, he tried harder to get the clearest, loudest sound possible. Besides, because of his hearing problem, he could concentrate on his work. He didn't have to worry about distractions from the outside world.

In 1877, while working on the telephone, Edison had another idea. If the human voice could be transmitted by means of a vibrating disk, he asked himself, why couldn't it also be recorded on some substance and reproduced later? He remembered that once, while working on a way to record the metallic taps of the telegraph on paraffin-coated tape wrapped around a cylinder, he had heard a musical sound when the tape was played back at a fast speed.

Edison's solution was a machine that had a cylinder set on a long shaft. He wrapped tinfoil around the cylinder, and at one end he placed a movable arm with a mouthpiece that had a thin disk with a needle at its tip. At the other end was a crank for turning the cylinder.

Edison's original phonograph, invented in 1877

Edison turned the cylinder at a steady speed and began to recite, "Mary had a little lamb/Its fleece was white as snow . . ." The sound waves of his voice made the disk vibrate, and as it did

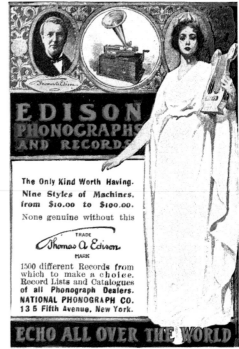

The phonograph, which Edison considered his greatest invention, became a huge success when it was made available to the public.

A later model of the Edison phonograph

so, the needle cut a groove on the tinfoil that was at some points shallow and at others deep, depending on the strength of the sound. When he had finished reciting the nursery rhyme, he returned the needle to the beginning of the groove. Then he turned the cylinder again. The needle made the disk vibrate, as it had done while recording, and the vibrations reproduced the original sound. The machine was talking! Edison's staff could hear his voice, weak but clear, repeating the poem.

The phonograph had been born. It would need many improvements, but Edison was no longer just a famous inventor. The phonograph made him a national hero, and he was invited to demonstrate his new machine at the White House before President Hayes.

A year later came the practical electric light, followed by years devoted to setting up electric power systems and companies in the United States and in Europe. Edison continued to work at the same pace, even though he was now a millionaire many times over.

In 1887, Edison moved to a larger laboratory at West Orange, New Jersey, where he built an electric locomotive. He did not develop this idea, however, because he was too busy with other projects. The automobile age had begun, and Edison wanted to build an electric car. He perfected a battery to power his car, but it was too expensive to develop commercially. Although he was the first to experiment with radio waves, he lost interest and thought radio had no future. His fertile mind continued to produce ideas at an astounding speed, but he could not possibly pursue all of them.

That same year, Edison began to think it would be possible to make a machine that does for the eye what the phonograph does for the ear. He knew that when a series of still photographs, each one showing a slight change in position, were shown quickly one after the other, the eye was tricked into seeing movement. He used this knowledge to develop a camera—which he called the Kinetograph—that could take a series of pictures on a roll of film. He also devised a projector—the Kinetoscope—to show the

Frames of film shot by Edison's Kinetograph

27

Top left: The first Kinetograph
Bottom left: The first Kinetoscope
Right: Edison operating the Kinetograph

pictures. He patented his invention in 1891 and began making short films showing boxers, acrobats, and dancers. The strange-looking structure where he shot the films—nicknamed the Black Maria—was the world's first motion-picture studio. Thus the motion picture had its beginnings not in Hollywood, but in New Jersey.

During the early 1890s, Edison focused on an unsuccessful project to extract iron from low-grade ore. But failure never dampened Edison's passion for invention, and even as he grew older, he continued to work hard. Between 1895 and 1927, he invented the flouroscope (enabling surgeons to perform America's first x-ray operation), developed an improved method for manufacturing cement, invented and perfected the alkaline storage battery (a battery that recharged itself), and experimented with natural substitutes for rubber.

In 1929, Edison's close friend Henry Ford arranged a celebration for the fiftieth anniversary of Edison's invention of the first practical electric light. It was held in Dearborn, Michigan, where Ford had set up a museum that included an exact reconstruction of Edison's Menlo Park laboratory. President Herbert Hoover, Orville Wright, Madame Marie Curie, and other important people from all over the world came to honor the eighty-two-year-old inventor. By this

Edison and Ford compare the first lightbulb with the 1929 version.

President Hoover (fourth from left) was among those who came to honor Edison at the fiftieth-anniversary celebration of the electric lightbulb.

Thomas and Mina Edison being interviewed outside their estate in 1931

time, Edison was ill with diabetes and kidney disease, and was no longer able to work. Two years later, on October 18, 1931, Thomas Alva Edison died at age eighty-four. At his death, he singly or jointly held 1,093 patents, more than any inventor in history.

Edison once recalled that as a boy he had seen covered wagons passing through his hometown in Ohio on their way west toward the California goldfields. Great herds of buffalo and Indian warriors still roamed the Great Plains, and the Pony Express was the speediest way to send a message.

When Thomas Edison died, America was a much different place. Electric lights now illuminated homes and businesses across the nation, and the marvelous devices he had invented or perfected had become commonplace.

In those eighty years, America had become the most technologically advanced nation in the world. It was no accident that all these changes took place during Edison's lifetime. For it was Thomas Edison's genius for invention that had created the electric age and had helped America gain its position. Edison's life was a perfect example of the American dream. He was a poor country boy who became a great success and helped people all over the world live better.

Edison in his laboratory in 1910

INDEX

PHOTO CREDITS

Picture Identifications:
Cover: Young Thomas Edison in his laboratory
Page 1: Edison listening to a phonograph in 1911
Page 2: Edison in his Menlo Park laboratory

Project Editor: Shari Joffe
Design: Karen Yops
Photo Research: Jan Izzo
Cornerstones of Freedom Logo: David Cunningham

ABOUT THE AUTHOR

Nicholas Nirgiotis has had many stories and articles published in magazines and newspapers. He is the author of *Erie Canal: Gateway to the West*. A graduate of the University of Chicago, Mr. Nirgiotis has been a teacher and a freelance writer. When not working, he likes to travel and read. Married, and the father of two sons, he lives in Wilmette, Illinois.